SOLO XTREME

9 X-traordinary and Challenging Piano Pieces

MELODY BOBER

The term "xtreme" is often used in sports to indicate feats that go beyond the ordinary. The pieces in Solo Xtreme were written to encourage students to achieve similar feats. Many pieces encountered by young pianists consist of single-line melodies that stay in one location on the keyboard. The pieces in this series move beyond this, challenging beginning students to change locations, cross hand-over-hand, play harmonic intervals and accidentals, use the pedal to create color and moods, and vary articulations. In addition, some suggest optional special effects using rhythm instruments. At the same time, they expand technique and musicianship.

In creating these pieces, I incorporated ideas that would encourage students to reach for new heights whether playing for their own enjoyment or for family and friends. The pieces also make impressive recital and contest solos. Enjoy!

Melody Bober

Contents

Festival Rag 2
Gentle Rain 6
Moonlight Skate 17
Ride Like the Wind 8
Roaming River 14
Rollerblade Race 20
Saturday Stomp 22
Sonoran Sunset 4
Twilight Echoes 11

Alfred Music
P.O. Box 10003
Van Nuys, CA 91410-0003
alfred.com

Copyright © 2017 Alfred Music
All rights reserved. Printed in USA.

ISBN-10: 1-4706-3867-3
ISBN-13: 978-1-4706-3867-2

Cover art:
Piano – spiral: © gettyimages.com / jennyhome • Snowboarder in Action: © gettyimages.com / Sportstock •
kiter's trick: © gettyimages.com / ohrimalex • Extreme Mountain Biker Jumping Off a Cliff: © gettyimages.com / MichaelSvoboda

Festival Rag

Melody Bober

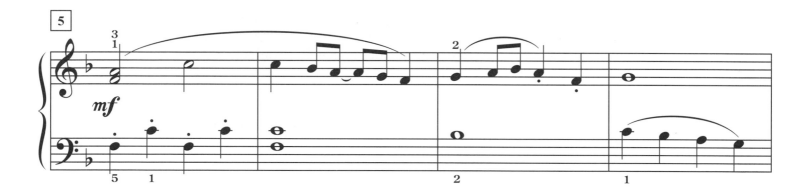

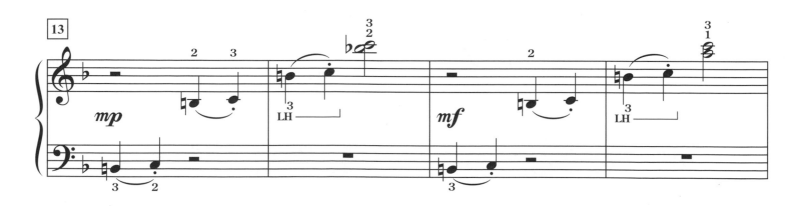

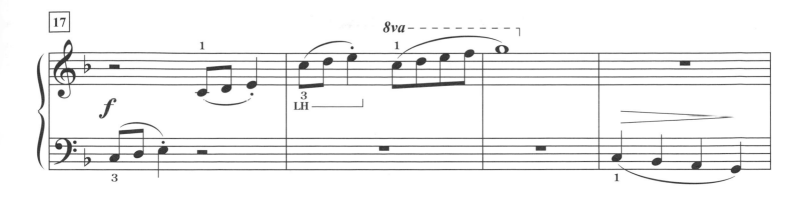

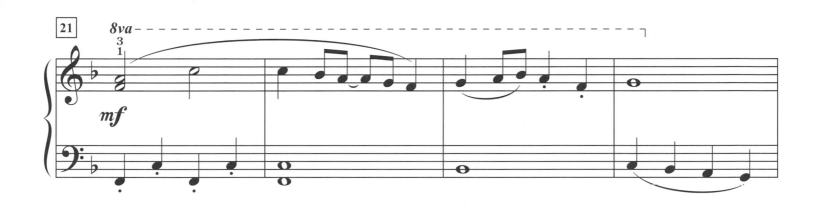

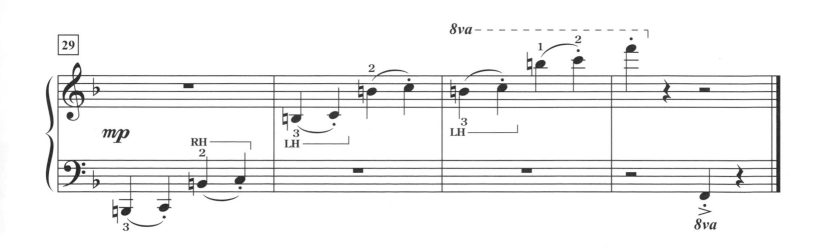

Sonoran Sunset

Melody Bober

Gentle Rain

Melody Bober

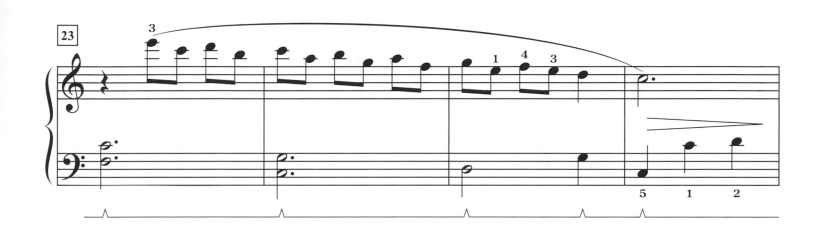

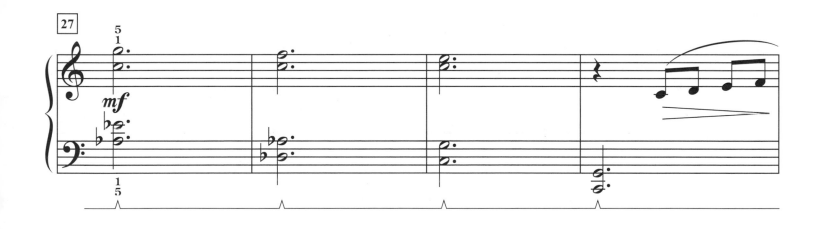

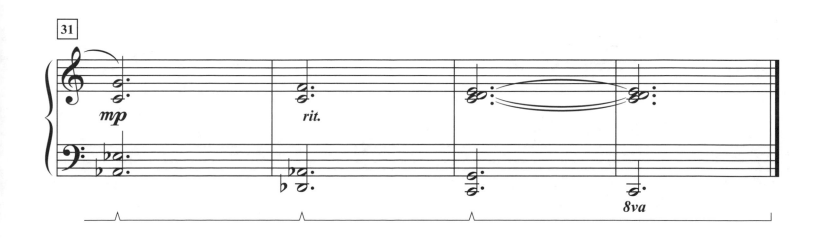

Ride Like the Wind

Melody Bober

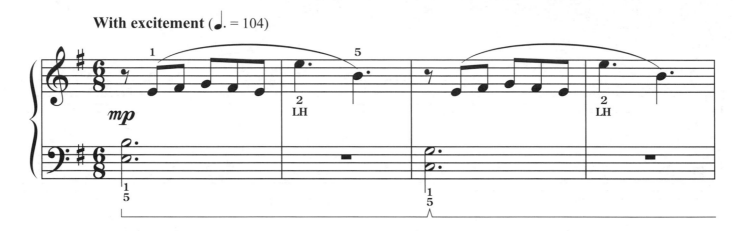

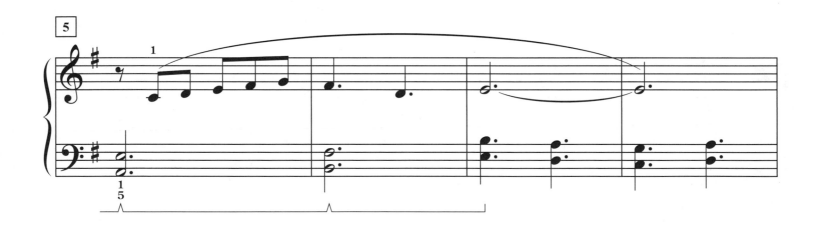

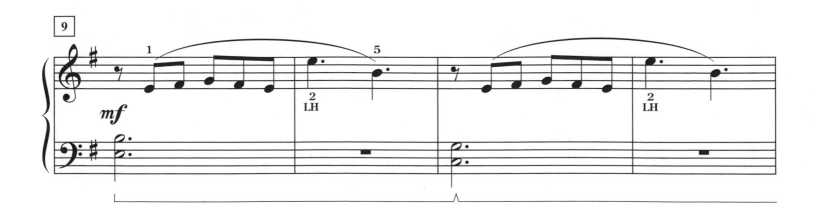

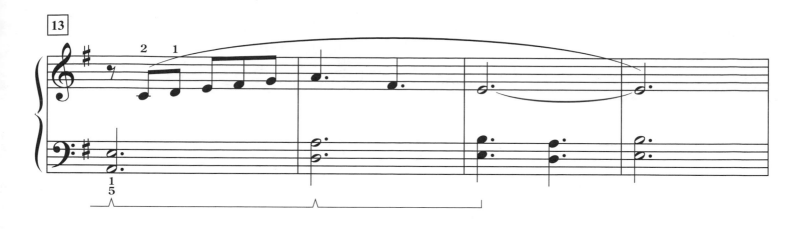

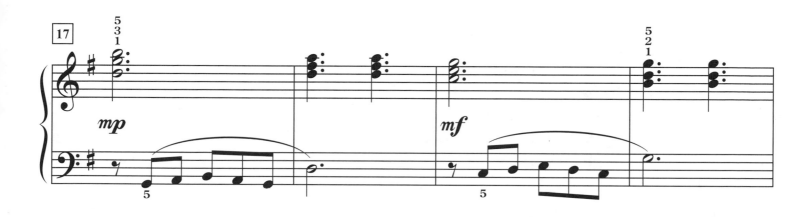

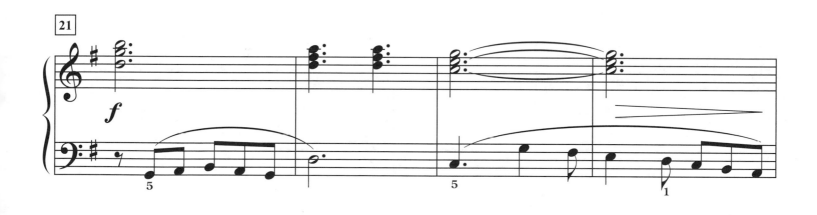

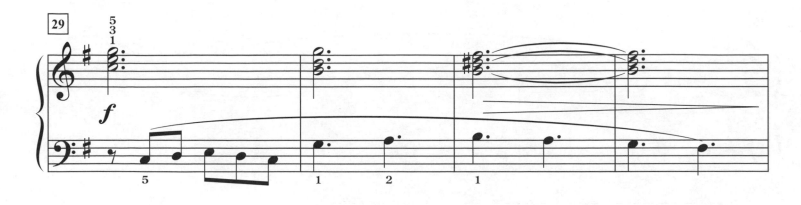

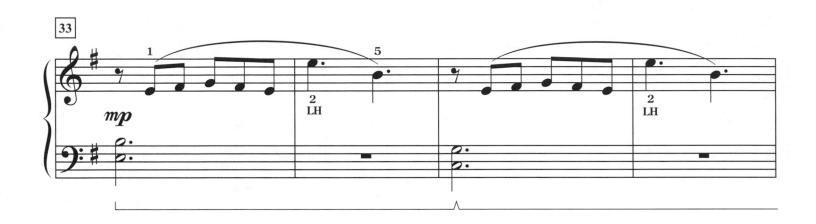

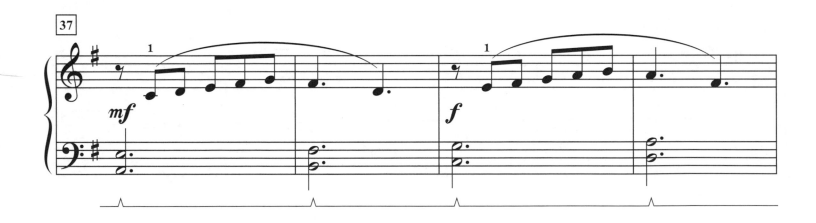

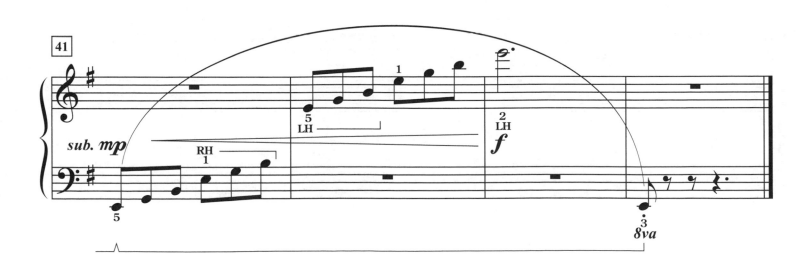

Twilight Echoes

Melody Bober

Roaming River

Melody Bober

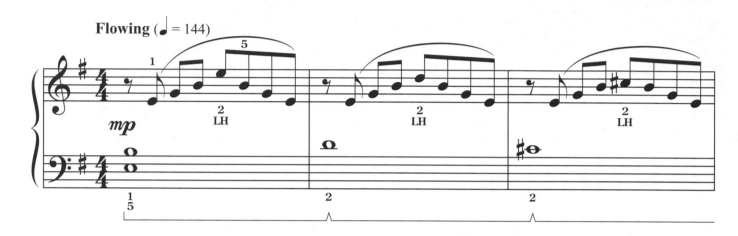

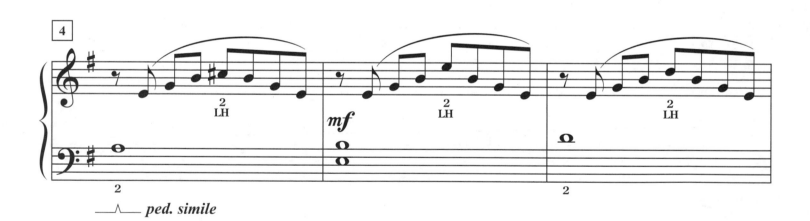

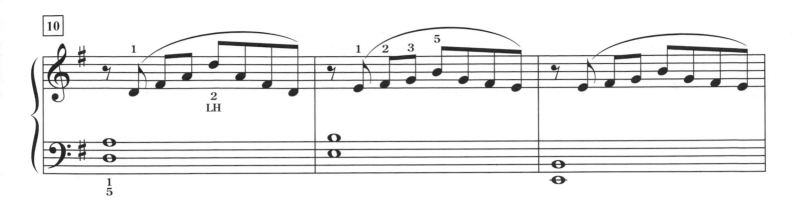

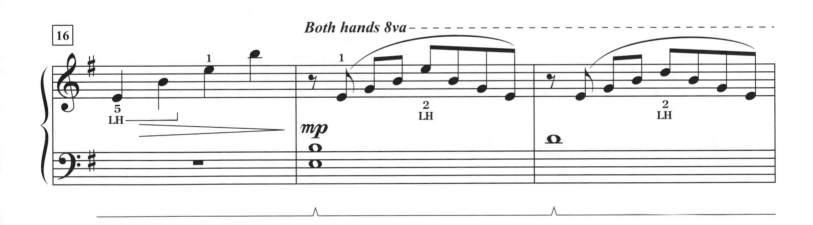

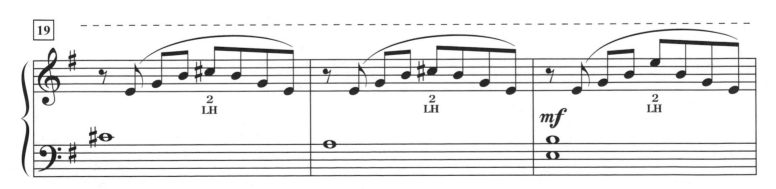

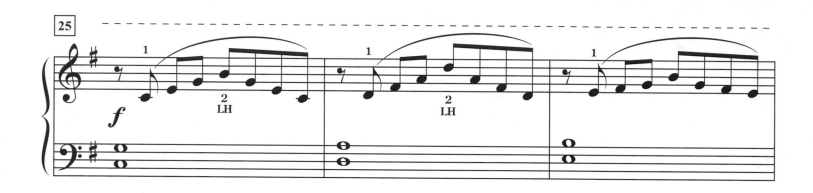

Moonlight Skate

Melody Bober

Rollerblade Race

Melody Bober

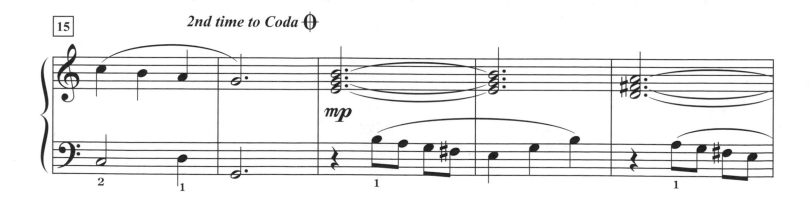

Saturday Stomp

Melody Bober